SWU-NAP- 010

UNIFORMS OF RUSSIAN ARMY DURING THE NAPOLEONIC WAR VOL.5

UNDER THE REIGN OF PAUL I
EMPEROR OF RUSSIA BETWEEN 1796 AND 1801
GUARDS INFANTRY AND CAVALRY

From the Viskovatov's greatest work:
"Historical description of the clothing and
arms of the Russian Army"

English translation by Mark Conrad

SOLDIERSHOP PUBLISHING

AUTHOR

Aleksandr Vasilevich Viskovatov born 22 April (4 May New Style) 1804, died 27 February (11 March) 1858 in St. Petersburg, Russian military historian. He graduated from the 1st Cadet Corps and served in the artillery, the hydrographic depot of the Naval Ministry, and then in the Department of Military Educational Institutions. He mainly studied historical artifacts and the histories of military units. Viskovatov's greatest work was the Historical Description of the Clothing and Arms of the Russian Army.

TRANSLATOR

Mark Conrad is an American historian with a great interest for all the Russian history.

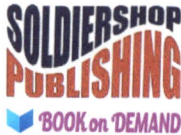

Title: **UNIFORMS OF RUSSIAN ARMY DURING THE NAPOLEONIC WAR VOL. 5 -
Guards Infantry and Cavalry 1 1796-1801**
By A. V. Viskovatov. English translation by Mark Conrad. First edition by Soldiershop.
Cover & Art Design: Luca S. Cristini. Plates re-colorations by Anna Cristini
ISBN code: 978-88-93270762

Published by Soldiershop publishing, via Padre Davide, 7 - 24050 Zanica (BG) ITALY. www.soldiershop.com

UNIFORMS
OF THE RUSSIAN
ARMY DURING THE
NAPOLEONIC WAR   VOL.5

UNDER THE REIGN OF PAUL I EMPEROR OF
RUSSIA BETWEEN 1796 AND 1801

*

Guards Infantry and Cavalry 1 1796-1801

HISTORICAL DESCRIPTION OF THE CLOTHING AND ARMS
OF THE RUSSIAN ARMY - A.V. VISKOVATOV
(First English translation by Mark Conrad)

Soldiershop is glad to presents the complete collection of the great job made by A.V. Viskovatov dedicated to the uniforms and weapons belonging to the Russian army during the Napoleonic period, until 1825. The time we considered corresponds to the reigns of two Tzars: Paul I, who reigned since 1769 until his murder on the 23rd of March 1801, and his son Aleksandr Pavlovi□ Romanov, that with the title of Alexander I, sat on the throne until the 1st December 1825.

Our reprint in based on the original 19th century volumes, to be precise the volumes from 7 to 9 are dedicated to the reign of Paul I; this first part is distributed on 7 volumes, having a numbering from 1 to 7. From number 10 to 18 of the original volumes, the second part is dedicated to the Russian troops under Alexander I. These still being worked on and they will be soon ready, distributed on twenty volumes approximately. Our new edition, the first ever published in English, both on paper and digital format, boasts a large number of color plates, many of them unpublished and coloured by our team of expert artists and scholars of uniformology. Each volume is based on 50/70 plates, always accompanied by the original translated text which describes the uniforms, the organization and the armament of the Russian army of the period.

A unique work in its genre, a must have in any respecting collection!
Aleksandr Vasilevich Viskovatov born 22 April (4 May New Style) 1804, died 27 February (11 March) 1858 in St. Petersburg, Russian military historian. He graduated from the 1st Cadet Corps and served in the artillery, the hydrographic depot of the Naval Ministry, and then in the Department of Military Educational Institutions.

He mainly studied historical artifacts and the histories of military units. Viskovatov's greatest work was the Historical Description of the Clothing and Arms of the Russian Army (Vols. 1-30, St. Petersburg, 1841-62; 2nd ed. Vols. 1-34, St. Petersburg - Novosibirsk - Leningrad, 1899-1948). This work is based on a great quantity of archival documents and contains four thousand colored illustrations.

Viskovatov was the author of Chronicles of the Russian Army (Books 1-20, St. Petersburg, 1834-42) and Chronicles of the Russian Imperial Army (Parts 1-7, St. Petersburg, 1852). He collected valuable material on the history of the Russian navy which went into A Short Overview of Russian Naval Campaigns and General Voyages to the End of the XVII Century (St. Petersburg, 1864; 2nd edition Moscow, 1946). Together with A.I. Mikhailovskii-Danilevskii he helped prepare and create the Military Gallery in the Winter Palace.

He wrote the historical military inscriptions for the walls of the Hall of St. George in the Great Palace of the Kremlin. (From the article in the Soviet Military Encyclopedia.)

CONTENTS

*

RUSSIAN ARMY,

Guards Infantry and Cavalry 1 1796-1801

Contents

Changes in the uniforms and equipment of the Guards, Military Educational Establishments, Cossack and National forces, various separate commands, and military personnel not part of the Army, from 1796 to 1801:

X. GUARDS INFANTRY (GVARDEISKAYA PEKHOTA)

The changes introduced by Emperor Paul I in the uniforms and armament of Army Infantry were also applied to the Guards Infantry, which consisted, as stated above, of three regiments: Preobrazhenskii, Semenovskii, and Izmailovskii, and of two battalions: Jäger and Garrison.

From 6 November 1796, when EMPEROR PAUL I ascended to the throne, to 3 December 1797 the musketeers (mushketery) of all three Life-Guards regiments wore a dark-green coat (kaftan) with fold-down collar: of red cloth in the Preobrazhenskii Regiment, blue (sinii) in the Semenovskii, and dark green in the Izmailovskii; with round or sewn (kruglyi ili sshivnyi) cuffs of red cloth, with lining of red kersey, and brass buttons. Vest (kamzol) and breeches (shtany) were white; everyday gaiters (vsednevnyya shtiblety) of black cloth, and white linen for parade dress; blunt-toed shoes; red neckcloth with white trim; hat with likewise white trim, a brass button, and three green tassels with their centers the color of the collar (Illus. 1119). Dark-green forage cap (furazhnaya shapka) with a red band or none, with trim in the color of the collar and a tassel in the company color, as for regiments of Army Infantry. Greatcoat (shinel') of dark-green cloth, with similar cinch, buttons, and fold-down collar. Warm coat (fufaika) for winter, of sheepskin. Weapons and accouterments, consisting of a rapier (shpaga) with a short-sword blade (tesachnyi klinok) and sword knot (temlyak), sword belt (portupeya), musket, frizzen cover (polunagalishche), cartridge pouch (patronnaya suma), knapsack (ranets), water flask (vodonosnaya flyazhka), and pouch for rusk (sukharnyi meshok), were all exactly like those for army musketeers.

Besides the color of the collar, regiments were distinguished one from the other by the color of the button loops (petlitsy) and tassels on the cuff flaps. These button loops were: Preobrazhenskii Regiment—yellow, with two red stripes; Semenovskii—yellow, with blue stripes; Izmailovskii—also yellow, with green stripes. There were also regimental differences in hair styles: in the first of these regiments the hair on the temple was gathered into three curls, in the second—into two, and in the third—into one (Illus. 1119) [1].

Non-commissioned officers in Musketeer companies had the same uniforms and weapons as private musketeers, but were distinguished from them in that: they had no shoulder straps on their coats; their hats had gold galloon; hat tassels and the ring around the sword knot were in three colors: white, orange, and black; white gloves with gauntlet cuffs; canes; and halberds (alebardy) instead of muskets. In the Izmailovskii Regiment these last items were the same as in the Army, but in the Preobrazhenskii and Semenovskii they were of a somewhat different pattern, like army officers' spontoons, with a spear point and socket 8 vershoks (14 inches) long (Illus. 1120) [(2) and (3)].

Drummers in Musketeer companies had the same uniform as private musketeers but were distinguished by swallows' nests (kryltsy) on the shoulders and chevrons (nashivki) sewn onto the sleeves, with the first item being the same color as the button loops on the cuff flaps and the tassels (Illus. 1121). Weapons, accouterments, and drums were the same as for army drummers, while drumsticks (barabannyya palki) were the same color as halberd shafts [(4)].

Privates in Grenadier companies—forming special Combined battalions (Svodnye bataliony) since 25 January 1797—were distinguished from musketeers in exactly the same way as in army regiments, but the front plate of the cap was gilded. The band was of gilded brass (iz mednoi, vyzolochennoi latuni) with three raised images of grenades and supports, and with dark-green cloth lining on the upper edge, while trim was narrow gold galloon with black silk. In the lower part of the cap plate the image of the Keizer-flag was colored with its prescribed red, blue, and white. On the sides of the plate, above the Keizer-flag, there was a single standard on the right, colored white, and on another, red, on the left, and on bother there was the Emperor's monogram in black paint. The rear sections of the caps were as in the Army, of cloth: red in the Preobrazhenskii Regiments; blue in the Semenovskii; and white in the Izmailovskii (Illus. 1122 and 1123) [(5)].

Master craftsmen on the establishment (frontovye masterovye) who were with the Grenadier companies were clothed and armed the same as grenadiers, but with the addition of an ax and leather apron (kozhanyi perednik ili zapon), colored, just as the ax carrier (toporishche), the same as halberd shafts [(6)].

Non-commissioned officers, drummers, and fifers in Grenadier companies, as well as regimental drummers and musicians (1 for a bassoon (faggot), 2 for clarinets (klarnety), and 2 for French horns (Waldhorns, valtorny)) were distinguished from the above lower combatant ranks by the same distinctions as prescribed in Army Musketeer regiments, as already described in detail above under the section for Army Infantry uniforms (Illus. 1124 and 1125) [(7)].

Company and field-grade officers and generals in Guards Infantry regiments were distinguished from lower ranks in the same way as in the Army Infantry, but with the addition of a gold tassel on the hat, after the example of officers of the Leib-Grenadier Regiment, mentioned above. In regard to colors, cuffs for all guards infantry regiment officers were of dark-green cloth; button loops on cuff flaps were embroidered in gold with a mixture of silk—red, sky blue, or green according to the regiment, with small tassels. As for collars, they were of red cloth in the Preobrazhenskii Regiment, of blue (sinii) velvet in the Semenovskii, and of dark-green cloth in the Izmailovskii (Illus. 1126). In addition, officers of the Semenovskii Regiment had gold aiguillettes (aksel'banty). Like the lower ranks, officers of all three regiments wore black gaiters for everyday use and white in parades. The shafts of their spontoons (espantony) were the same as for halberds [(8)].

Noncombatant lower ranks: chaplain's assistants (tserkovniki), medics (fel'dshery), gunstock makers (lozhniki), the gunsmith (ruzheinyi master), the gunstock maker's andgunsmith's apprentices (ucheniki), farrier (konoval), blacksmiths (kuznetsy), carpenter (plotnik), provost (profos), train personnel (furleity), and also from 1797 the wagon master (vagenmeister) were all prescribed the same uniforms as these ranks had in Army Infantry regiments [9].

Noncombatant officers: quartermasters (kvartermistry), legal experts (auditory), and doctors (lekarya) also had the same uniforms as quartermaster, legal assistants, and doctors in the Army Infantry [10].

3 January 1797 – The inscription "1700 No 19" on company-grade officers' gorgets in the Preobrazhenskii and Semenovskii regiments, as granted by EMPEROR PETR I, is removed [11].

3 December 1797 – When the foot regiments of the Life-Guards were organized as: Preobrazhenskii—one Grenadier and three Musketeer battalions, and the Semenovskii and Izmailovskii—one Grenadier and two Musketeer battalions, the uniforms of these regiments underwent the following changes:

1) The wide fall-down collar on coats in the Izmailovskii Regiment were changed to narrow and standing (Illus. 1127, 1128, and 1129).

2) All combatant ranks of the three regiments were ordered to have slit cuffs, black neckcloths, and gold button loops on the collar and cuffs. The button loops had stripes (red, blue, and green, by regiment) and tassels: of galloon for lower ranks and embroidered for officers (Illus. 1127, 1128, and 1129)[12].

3) Officers were given red cuffs instead of dark green, and hats with wide toothed gold galloon, a cockade, and a button loop, i.e. similar to those for generals but without plumage on the edges. Also, officers of the Preobrazhenskii and Izmailovskii, to make them the same as in the Semenovskii, were given gold aiguillettes (Illus. 1129) [13].

4 December 1797 – With the reorganization of the Life-Guards Preobrazhenskii Regiment into two Grenadier and three Musketeer battalions, in the first Grenadier battalion, or Leib-Battalion, the backs of caps were directed to be yellow, and in the second Grenadier battalion—red. In this same year, officers and lower ranks of the Izmailovskii Regiment had their curls cut off [14].

2 January 1798 – In the Leib-Battalion of the Izmailovskii Regiment the shafts of halberds and spontoons were ordered to be coffee colored (kofeinyi), the same color as the flag poles [15].

16 December 1798 – Upon the occasion of EMPEROR PAUL I assuming the title of Grand Master of the Order of St. John of Jerusalem, it was ordered that on the front plates of grenadier caps the image of the Keizer-flag be replaced by a white cross on a red field (Illus. 1130a), and following this there be added to the medallions on officers' gorgets the white cross of St. John of Jerusalem, surrounded by a gold border and topped by a gold crown (Illus. 1130b) [16].

6 January 1799 – In the second and third battalions of the Semenovskii Regiment the shafts of halberds and spontoons were ordered to be white, and in the same battalions of the Izmailovskii Regiment—black. In the first battalions of these regiments and in all the battalions of the Preobrazhenskii, they were coffee-colored, as before. Later these colors changed once more, namely—in the Leib-Battalion of the Preobrazhenskii Regiment the shafts were coffee, and in the other battalions—yellow; in the Semenovskii—black; in the Izmailovskii—white [17].

10 August 1799 – Guards grenadier caps were given plates of a new pattern, of the same size as before but with a large black two-headed eagle on whose breast was a white cross on a raspberry shield with a gold edge. On the upper part of the plate, between the crown and the eagle, is

EMPEROR PAUL I's monogram, and above the crown the word "Blagodat" ("Blessed") in raised Cyrillic letters. The very same eagle and inscription are stamped at the read of the headband, and the band itself is somewhat changed and larger than before (Illus. 1131)[18]. Along with this the yellow color for the rear of grenadier caps in the First, or Leib, Battalion of the Preobrazhenskii Regiment was replaced by raspberry, while the red of the Second Battalion—by yellow [19].

9 October 1799 – The top of the knot on officers' sashes and the top of their sword knots, and the tops of hat tassels, as well as of lower ranks' sword knots, were ordered to be raspberry. The stripes on sashes and the tassels of hats, sword knots, and sashes were to be tricolored: black, orange, and raspberry [20].

March 1800 – When the Life-Guards Preobrazhenskii Regiment was organized into five battalions, and the Semenovskii and Izmailovskii into three Grenadier battalions, all of these regiments were ordered to have:

1) Lower combatant ranks – cuffs round instead of slit; no buttons on the cuffs, but above them on the flaps; red neckcloth with white trim (Illus. 1132) [21].

In the First, or Leib, Battalion of the Preobrazhenskii Regiment – red backs to the grenadier caps, plates and cap bands of gilded brass, with painted eagles as established on 10 August 1799, white tuft (Illus. 1133a); in the Second Battalion – yellow backs to the caps, plates and cap bands the same as in the preceding battalion, red tuft (Illus. 1133b); in the Third – red backs to the caps, brass plates with unpainted eagles, cap band of blue cloth, with three grenades, blue tuft (Illus. 1133c); in the Fourth – red backs to the caps, plates with painted eagles, cap band of yellow cloth, with three grenades, yellow tuft (Illus. 1133d); in the Fifth – red backs to the caps, plates with unpainted eagles, cap band of dark-green cloth, with three gilded grenades, dark-green tuft (Illus. 1133e); in the Leib-Battalion of the Semenovskii Regiment – blue backs to the caps, plate and cap band of gilded brass, with a painted eagle as in the Leib-Battalion of the Preobrazhenskii Regiment, white tuft with a blue center (Illus. 1133f); in the Second – blue backs to the caps, plate with an unpainted eagle, white cap band, with three grenades, white tuft with a blue center (Illus. 1133g); in the Third – blue backs to the caps, plate with an unpainted eagle, red cap band, with three grenades, red tuft with a blue center (Illus. 1133h); in the Leib-Battalion of the Izmailovskii Regiment – white backs to the caps, plate and cap band of gilded brass, with a painted eagle as in the Leib-Battalions of the Preobrazhenskii and Semenovskii regiments, white tuft with a green center (Illus. 1133i); in the Second – white backs to the caps, plate with an unpainted eagle, dark-green cap band, with three grenades, white tuft with a green center (Illus. 1133k); in the Third – white backs to the caps, plate with an unpainted eagle, dark-green cap band, with three grenades, red tuft with a green center (Illus. 1133l). As previously, trim on the gilded plates was gold with black silk, and on brass plates—yellow worsted, with black [22].

3) For officers of the Preobrazhenskii Regiment – coats with narrow fold-down red collars, red lapels and slit cuffs, with gold embroidery along the edges of the lapels, cuffs, and cuff flaps, across the lapels and flaps above the cuffs, and on the waistline (Illus. 1134 and 1135, a) [23].

4) For officers of the Semenovskii and Izmailovskii regiments – coats with round cuffs and gold embroidery on the collar, down the front opening, on the cuffs, cuff flaps, and waistline (Illus. 1134 and 1135, b and c) [24].

5) For officers of all three regiments – white neckcloths, hats with narrow gold galloon and a tassel,

without a cockade or button loops (Illus. 1135) [25].

At the end of 1800, officers of the Preobrazhenskii Regiment were ordered to have embroidery of a new pattern, with tassels exactly like those prescribed for officers of the Semenovskii and Izmailovskii regiments, and round cuffs (Illus. 1135d and 1136) [26].

At the same time there was a change in the uniforms for fifers in the Life-Guards Preobrazhenskii Regiment. They were given dark-green cloth coats with red collar, cuffs, and lining, the skirts turned up a little, gold galloon on all seams, and a wide belt of red stamin (stamed), sewn so that in front it was flat when fastened and in back gathered into a bow with two hanging ends. Also, instead of hats, they received red cloth caps wound at the bottom with white linen in the style of a Turkish chalma, or turban, and decorated with a white plume similar to those used by hussar generals at the time. This plume was inserted into a tube fixed to the front of the cap and covered with a elongated convex gilded plate (Illus. 1137) [27].

When in formation, one of the regimental musicians carried a Turkish drum (Turetskii baraban) as introduced into Russia at the time, painted in red and black checks with white edging between them (Illus. 1138). Both in height and in diameter this drum measured 14 vershoks (24 1/2 inches) [28].

Life-Guards Jäger Battalion: privates, non-commissioned officers, waldhornists, staff-waldhornists, field and company-grade officers, a general, and all noncombatants, during the whole of EMPEROR PAUL I's reign had uniforms and armaments that were exactly the same as for army jägers. The collar, cuffs, and aiguillette for this battalion's lower ranks were light orange, and buttons were yellow (Illus. 1139). For waldhornists – lace chevrons, the lace being gold with red tracery (Illus. 1140). For officers – aiguillettes, and gold galloon on the hat (Illus. 1141) [29].

Life-Guards Garrison Battalion: grenadiers, non-commissioned officers, company and battalion drummers, fifers, musicians (1 for the bassoon, 2 for clarinets, and 2 for the French horn, or waldhorn), and noncombatants such as lazaret attendants, medics, gunstock maker, metal smith, and—ranked as an officer—the doctor, had, for the whole of EMPEROR PAUL I's reign since the establishment of this battalion on 29 July 1799, uniforms, accouterments, and weapons like those confirmed for the Life-Guards Preobrazhenskii Regiment on 3 and 16 December 1797, but without button loops and with the following changes: white buttons instead of white, silver plates on the grenadier caps instead of gilded, and silver officers' aiguillettes instead of gold (Illus. 1142) [40]. The orders of 10 August and 9 October 1799 regarding new plates for grenadier caps and the addition of raspberry coloring to hat tassels, sword knots, and sashes were extended with equal force to the Life-Guards Garrison Battalion [31]. The backs of grenadier caps in this battalion were dark green and the trim was silk—silver with black, and the tuft was blue (sinii) with a yellow center (Illus. 1142) [32].

Russian grenadiers of the Guard. 1800 about

XI. GUARDS CAVALRY (GVARDEISKAYA KAVALERIYA)

With the ascension of EMPEROR PAUL I to the Throne, the Cavalier Guards Corps, established in 1762, kept the same uniform clothing and weapons that it had during the preceding reign, up to its disbandment on 6 December 1796.

The new Cavalier Guards Corps, first formed as a single squadron on 11 November 1796 and later reorganized as two and then three squadrons—existing in this last form until 30 October 1797 under the title of Cavalier Guards squadrons—received uniforms and weapons of the patterns established by EMPEROR PAUL I for Cuirassier regiments.

Chevalier Guards privates (ryadovye kavalergardy) had: kolet coat of white kersey with red cloth collar and cuffs, with trim down the front and on the skirts of three-stripe lace— silver in the center and red along the sides—and with silver galloon on the collar and cuffs; vest (kamzol) of red cloth with the same trim as on the coat; hat (shlyapa) with tassels of silver and red silk (iz serebra and krasnago shelka, i.e. silver is a noun, not an adjective like "red" – M.C.); red cloth cover to the sabertache, with straight silver galloon along th edges, and with a white star in the center, after the example of the stars on the sabertaches of the two Leib-Cuirassier regiments; red girdle (kushak); broadsword (palash), with a silvered hilt, steel scabbard, and black silk sword knot with a silver tassel; carbine with deerskin strap trimmed on its upper surface with silver galloon; cartridge pouch (lyadunka) with silvered badge; cross strap (pogonnaya perevyaz') and cartridge-pouch strap (lyadunochnyi remen'), trimmed with red cloth and—in the the center—silver galloon; shabrack (cheprak) and pistol carriers (chushki) of red cloth with narrow silver galloon along the edges, and with the same stars as on the sabertache. All other items were the same as for cuirassiers (Illus. 1143) [33].

Non-commissioned officers (unter-ofitsery), including officer candidates (estandart-yunkera), had a mix of black and orange silk in the tassels of their hats and sword knots, and the top of their plumes were a mix of black and orange feathers. Also, they did not wear cartridge pouches (Illus. 1444) [34].

Trumpeters, staff-trumpeters, and the kettledrummer (trubachi, shtab-trubachi i litavrshchik), in addition to the same distinctions as these ranks had in Cuirassier regiments, had silver lace with red edging sewn on their clothing (Illus. 1145) [35].

Officers wore coats with wide toothed silver galloon and waistcoats with narrow flat-edge silver galloon. They had wide silver galloon with a fringe on their shabracks and pistol carriers, and similarly silver stars (Illus. 1146) [36].

Non-combatant lower ranks: chaplain's assistants, medics, barbers, clerks, gunstock makers and gunsmith, saddle maker and his apprentices, tub mender ("fanshmit" – c.f German Wanne meaning "tub" – M.C.), metalsmiths, blacksmiths, farriers, carpenters, provost, train personnel, and also the stablemaster, quartermaster, legal expert (auditor), and doctor, were uniformed like the corresponding ranks in Cuirassier regiments [37].

On parade, all combatant ranks, officers as well as lower ranks, wore black supervests (supervesty) with toothed white shoulder pieces and red trim along which was sewn silver cord (Illus. 1147 and 1148). For lower ranks these supervests were of cloth with worsted velvet (tripovyi) trim, and for officers both the vest and trim were velvet (barkhatnyi). Furthermore, in parade uniform, all straps of officers' horse furniture were trimmed with red worsted velvet, and on the trim were thin gold cords. Buckles, fastenings, fixtures, and all decorative bosses were gilded (Illus. 1149) [38].

At EMPEROR PAUL I's coronation and some other ceremonial occasions at the HIGHEST COURT, cavalier guards wore armor plates (laty) over their supervests, two skirt-like attachments (poly) on the front one of these; silver gauntlets (naruchniki) and thigh pieces (nabedrenniki); silver shishak helmets and white knightly sashes (sharfy) over the right shoulder. The armor plates consisted of two halves: a front or breast plate, and a back plate, with a black two-headed eagle on whose breast was a red shield with gold edges. On the shield was an image of St. George with gold crown, beak, claws, scepter, and orb. There were gilded rivets and red worsted velvet trim (velvet for officers) (Illus. 1150). The component parts of the skirts, gauntlets, and thigh pieces were held together by gilt rivets. The shishak helmets had red ostrich feathers for lower ranks and white for officers, and a gilt eagle and rivets (Illus. 1151 and 1152). Lower ranks' sashes had a white fringe, while those of officers had a silver fringe [39].

6 April 1799 – The Cavalier Guards Corps, newly established as a personal Guard for the Grand Master of the Order of St. John of Jerusalem, was given uniforms of the same pattern as those described above for Cavalier Guard squadrons, but with kolet coats with black plissé collar, cuffs, and trim on the small skirts, and with gold galloon. Waistcoats were of black cloth without galloon. Hats had two silk cockades, one laid on top of the other: the smaller was of white ribbon with a red edge, while the larger was of black with orange edging; gold buttonhole loop, button, and tassels; a plume of white feathers, red at the base. Girdles (kushaki) of raspberry stamin, with a fringe. Sabertache cover of black plissé, with gold galloon around the edges and a likewise gold embroidered crown, and with a similarly embroidered silver cross of St. John of Jerusalem. This cross was also on the hat's buttonhole loop and button. All straps for the sword belt and sabertache were of red morocco and picked out along the edges with white thread, while the carbine strap was of red Russian leather. Broadswords and sword knots were the same as in 1797. The crossbelt had a gilt buckle, fastener, and end piece, an iron hook, and trim in the form of three raspberry worsted velvet stripes and two gold stripes. The pouch had a brass star with a silver cross of the order on it. The pouch belt was trimmed along its edges with raspberry worsted velvet and down its middle with gold galloon. The shabrack and pistol holders were of white cloth with gold galloon and silver embroidered stars under gold crowns (Illus. 1153) [40].

Noncommissioned officers had the same uniforms as private cavalier guardsmen but with silver tassels on the hat. In regard to weaponry there were the same differences as described above for cavalier guards in 1797 (Illus. 1154) [41].

The coats of trumpeters and the kettledrummer and the swallows' nests customary for these ranks, trimmed with gold galloon. Hats had red worsted tassels and red hair trim (krasnyi, volosyanoi plyumazh). Sword knots of red morocco, with a red worsted tassel (Illus. 1154). Trumpets and kettledrums were silver, the latter with gold tassels [42].

Officers had the same distinctions compared to private cavalier guardsmen as in 1797, but with the addition of wide toothed galloon and white plumage trim on their hats, and with the usual silver officers' sashes exchanged for gold ones with raspberry silk and silver stripes along the edges, in which was inserted orange and black silk (Illus. 1155) [43].

In parade order, cavalier guardsmen, their noncommissioned officers, trumpeters, and the kettledrummer all wore supervests of raspberry worsted velvet, with the cross of the order of St. John of Jerusalem made from white Manchester cloth, and with silver galloon along the edges (Illus. 1156). Officers' supervests were velvet with a silver cross (Illus. 1156)[44].

During grand ceremonies (bol'shiya torzhestva), all combatant ranks of the Cavalier Guards Corps wore black lacquered helmets (kaski) with gilt visor, eagle, comb, and rivets, and with ostrich feathers: red for lower ranks and white for officers (Illus. 1157 and 1158). Along with the helmets, order sashes (ordenskie sharfy) were worn over the right shoulder, of raspberry silk with a fringe that for lower ranks was again raspberry, but for officers—gold. Swordknots were also raspberry [45].

When off duty, cavalier guardsmen and non-commissioned officers wore an undress uniform (vitse-mundir) consisting of a red cloth coat (kaftan) cut in dragoon style, with collar, lapels, and cuffs of black plissé. It had white lining and the same buttons as on the hat, and was worn with a gold aiguilette on the right shoulder and a gold epaulette on the left. With this was worn white waistcoats and broadswords with scabbards in the pattern for dragoons, with a silver sword knot, while an infantry-style swordbelt with frog was worn under the waistcoat (Illus. 1159) [46].

The undress coat for trumpeters was similar to that for cavalier guardsmen but with swallows' nests and raspberry and black worsted tape (bason) sewn on in the same manner as on the coats of dragoon trumpeters (Illus. 1159) [47].

The kettledrummer's undress coat was the same as for trumpeters, but without swallows' nests [48]. Officers had an undress coat with velvet collar, lapels, and cuffs, and were further distinguished from plain cavalier guardsmen in that their hats had galloon and plumage trim (Illus. 1160) [49].

Besides the uniforms described above, all lower combatant ranks of the Cavalier Guards Corps were prescribed dark-green cloth frock coats (sertuki) and greatcoats (shineli). The first had a black plissé collar while the latter's was of red cloth. Officers also wore dark-green frock coats, but with collars of black velvet [50].

Non-combatant ranks: medics, clerks, gunsmith and metal smith, saddle maker, farrier, and also the stablemaster and staff-doctor—all kept the previous uniforms as used throughout the cavalry [51].

In the beginning of the year 1800, all ranks in the Cavalier Guards Corps were wearing supervests with an order cross to which was added embroidered gold lilies (Illus. 1161). At this time undress coats had their lapels and gold aiguilettes removed, and the buttons were changed to silver (Illus. 1162) [52].

From 15 May 1800, when the Cavalier Guards Corps was reorganized into the three-squadron Cavalier Guards Regiment, its ranks were given the following uniform clothing, which was kept by them during the entire remainder of EMPEROR PAUL I's reign:

Cavalier guardsmen – kolet coat, of straw-colored kersey, with red cloth collar, cuffs, trim along the front opening and skirts, and shoulder straps, all trimed with raspberry and black wool tape. Two buttonhole loops of this same tape were on each cuff; waistcoat – of red cloth, also with tape; hat and supervest – of the same pattern as laid down in 1799 for the Cavalier Guards Corps, except the latter was red instead of raspberrry; girdle of red stamin. The crossbelt and pouch belt were trimmed with red cloth on which was the same tape as on the coat; cartridge pouches – with a white stamped and forged star, in the center of which was laid a black two-headed eagle; sabertache, shabrack, and pistol holders - of red cloth with two rows of tape, also the same as on the coat, and with stars the same as on the cartridge pouch (Illus. 1163). In addition to the clothing described above, cavalier guardsmen werer also authorized white smocks (kiteli) and similarly white forage caps: the first of calamanco, and the second of cloth, with a red band, piping, and tassel [53].

Non-commissioned officers and officer candidates (estandart-yunkera) had gold galloon along the edge of the collar and cuffs, and similarly gold buttonhole loops on the cuffs (Illus. 1164) [54].

Trumpeters and staff-trumpeters wore coats with swallows' nests and sewn-on trim of the same tape as on the coats of private cavalier guardsmen, while their hats had red hair trim (Illus. 1164) [55]. The kettledrummer was prescribed a coat without swallows' nests [56].

Officers had coats of straw-colored cloth with puce velvet, and with gold galloon sewn on in the same places as the tape for privates. They also had a gold aiguilette; waistcoat trimmed with gold galloon; sash – silver with black, orange, and raspberry silk; velvet supervests; shabrack and pistol holders – with gold galloon and black eagles on silver stars (Illus. 1165) [57]. At grand parades, lower ranks had red worsted velvet (trip) on their uniforms and accouterments instead of red cloth, and instead of tape—gold galloon [58].

The undress coat was kept only for officers, and was, as before, of red cloth with a small standing collar, also of red cloth. It had lapels and slit cuffs of black cloth, a silver aiguilette, and similarly silver embroidered buttonhole loops: fourteen on the lapels, eight on the cuffs, and eight on the skirts (Illus. 1166) [59].

During the whole of of EMPEROR PAUL I's reign, the Life-Guards Horse Regiment had uniform clothing, weapons, and horse furniture of the patterns for cuirassiers, with all the features that distinguished ranks within the regiment.

From November 1796, lower combatant ranks had red cloth collars and cuffs on their coats; tape was of red worsted velvet; waistcoat – dark blue; sabertache cover, shabrack, and pistol holders – dark blue, with the same small stars as for leib-cuirassiers; girdles according to the squadron: red in the Leib-Squadron, yellow in the second, dark blue in the third, green in the fourth, and black in the fifth (Illus. 1167, 1168, and 1169). Trim on the skirts or turnbacks (Obkladki na polkakh ili faldakh) of officers' coats were in these same colors, while appointments were gold (Illus. 1170 and 1171). Trumpets and kettledrums remained silver as before [60]. Officers also had a red cloth undress coat (vitse-mundir) with collar and cuffs of dark-blue cloth and lining, lining the same color as the trim on the kolet coat's skirts, and gild buttons, while the waistcoat worn with this undress coat was white (Illus. 1172) [61].

From November 1797, with the disbandment of the Cavalier Guard squadrons, their shishak helmets and armor were transferred to the Horse Regiment of the Life Guards, part of which now appeared at grand ceremonies with silk sashes worn over the right shoulder. At first these were white with raspberry stripes, but later they were completely raspberry. Both styles had silver fringes [62].

At the beginning of 1799, the dark blue of the L.-Gds. Horse Regiment's waistcoats, sabertaches, shabracks, and pistol carriers was changed to black, and officers were given a raspberry undress coat with a black velvet collar and cuffs and gold embroidery (Illus. 1173 and 1174) [63].

9 October 1799 – The knots (shishki) of officers' sashes, swordknots, and hat tassels, as well as of lower ranks' swordknots, were ordered to be raspberry. The stripes on sashes and in the tassels of

hats, swordknots, and sashes were to be of three colors: black, orange, and raspberry [64].

2 February 1800 – The black waistcoats, sabertaches, shabracks, and pistol carriers of the regiment's combatant ranks were again changed to dark blue, and officers' undress coats were ordered to be without embroidery, with dark-blue collar, cuffs, and lining, i.e. except for the color of the lining, the same in all respects as the undress coats of 1796 and 1797 [65]. A little later, Horse Guards officers were given the exact same undress coat as officers of the Cavalier Guards received in 1800, but with dark-blue lapels and cuffs instead of black, and with gold buttons and buttonhole loops instead of silver [66].

Leib Hussars (Leib-gusary), from 13 December 1797, had two uniforms: everyday and parade (vsednevnoe i paradnoe). Both the one and the other were of the pattern authorized for army hussars.

The parade uniform for Leib Hussar privates consisted of: green cloth pelisse (mentiya) trimmed with black sable fur and lined with black astrakhan; crimson cloth dolman (dulmanka); and cloth breeches (shtany), green at the top and crimson below. All three had cord trim and lace of white worsted and buttons of English tin. The Leib hussars wore short boots (sapogi) reaching below the knee, with a notch cut out in front and white worsted cord trim around the edge; neckcloth of black flannel; deerskingloves, with gauntlet cuffs; headdress (shapka) of raccoon fur colored black, with a crimson cloth bag, white plume, and white worsted tassels and cords; girdle (poyas) of green worsted with slides or barrels and tassels of white worsted (Illus. 1175). The top of the sabertache was of crimson cloth, with a black eagle on whose breast was a white shield, and a straw-colored monogram and crown, all of cloth, and with white worsted tape and cord piping; crimson cloth saddle cloth (valtrap) with notched green cloth trim, and with white worsted tape, cord piping, and monograms. Everything else, which is to say sword belt, saber, sword knot, carbine, cartridge pouch with strap, saddle, and all horse furniture in general, with its appurtenences, were of the same patterns as those for army hussars [67]. Non-commissioned officers—who, as in the army, were not authorized the carbine and cartridge-pouch belt—were further distinguished from privates in having a cane and silver galloon on the collar, cuffs, and along the buttons of the pelisse and dolman (Illus. 1176) [68]. Trumpeters were distinguished from privates, and staff-trumpeters from non-commissioned officers, by sewn-on stripes of crimson and silver worsted velvet tape, with swallows' nests, and furthermore by the cord braid on their pelisses being white with crimson, and on the dolman—white with green (Illus. 1176) [69]. For officers, all cord, lace, and buttons were silver; plumes—of the style worn by hussar generals, with wings and a tube holding the plume; instead of a pelisse—"panthers" ("barsy"), i.e. a panther skin lined with red ratine (ratin) and trimmed around with silver galloon, with silver claws at the ends of the paws (Illus. 1177 and 1178). These panther skins were worn head down, with the right front paw thrown over the left shoulder and the right back paw passed under the right arm and then the both of them fastened by the claws to a round silver medalion (medalion) decorated with the gold IMPERIAL monogram under a similarly gold crown. In this way the remaining two paws of the panther were left hanging, and the tail was thrown behind the right rear paw. The saddle cloth (valtrap) was red with silver galloon and cord, and had similarly silver embroidered monograms. Part of leib-hussar officers' horse furniture was additional black leather sarsam decoration, plaited from thin, narrow straps (Illus. 1177 and 1179)[70].

For everyday use, combatant ranks wore white deerskin chakchiry pants without any decoration, and boots without any trim (Illus. 1180). Non-commissioned officers and trumpeters, instead of hussar headgear, wore standard cavalry hats (Illus. 1180). Officers, instead of the panther skins, wore the same pelisses prescribed for lower ranks, but with white fox fur trim (opushka iz belago, lis'yago mekha) and silver appointments instead of worsted. Their hats had plain plumes without the tube or wing (Illus. 1181). Like army hussars, Leib-Hussar officers also wore vengerki ("Hungarian") coats of green cloth with silver trim and red lining (Illus. 1182) [71].

Non-combatant ranks were uniformed following the example of non-combatants in the Army and heavy Guards Cavalry. All except wagon drivers (izvoshchiki) and provosts (profosy)—who had dark-green greatcoats (shineli)—wore white cloth cloaks (plashchi) that were also prescribed for combatant ranks. Forage caps in the Leib-Hussar Regiment were white with a red band, and with a tassel in the squadron color [72].

1798 July 10 – Leib-Hussar trumpeters' sewn-on lace—formerly of red worsted velvet with silver—was replaced with entirely silver lace. White cloaks were kept only for combatant hussars, and all non-combatants were prescribed dark-green greatcoats [73].

1798 October 13 – Each Leib-Hussar squadron was ordered to have 16 musketoons (mushkatony) with a barrel 17 1/2-inches (10 vershok) long, but otherwise the same fittings as for carbines [74].

1798 October 19 – For parades and ceremonial and victory days, officers and lower ranks of the two squadrons of the Leib-Hussar Regiment were ordered to have panther skins and plumes with tubes and wings [75].

1799 January 1 – The Leib-Hussar Regiment was given white pelisses and dolmans, with straw-colored (palevye) collars and cuffs; white chakchiry pants of deerskin; white sabertaches and saddlecloths with straw-colored trim; all cord, galloon, tassels, and buttons – yellow. Officers' appointments were gold (Illus. 1183) [76].

1799 January 31– Leib-Hussars' cloaks were replaced with greatcoats of the same pattern as for army cavalry [77].

1799 October 9 – Leib-Hussar officers were ordered to add raspberry silk to the black and orange silk of their sword knots, waistbelts, and tassels on caps and hats [78].

1799 October 20 – The white cloth of Leib-Hussar Regiment pelisses, dolmans, sabertaches, and saddlecloths was replaced with raspberry. The fur caps in use were replaced by black cloth shakos (kivera) similar to those used under EMPRESS CATHERINE II: for lower ranks—with yellow worsted trim, and for officers—with gold trim (Illus. 1184) [79].

1800 June 11 – Gloves were withdrawn from privates in the Leib-Hussar Regiment, and company-grade officers and non-commissioned officers were ordered to have them without gauntlet cuffs [80].

From 1796 December 13, Leib-Cossacks had crimson cloth half-caftans (polukaftan'ya) which they wore tucked into turquoise cloth shirovary pants. Their boots, as for all troops, had blunt toes. Their neckcloths were of black foulard silk (fler). Headdresses (shapki) were of black Bukhara fleece with scarlet cloth bags; cords and tassels were of sky-blue and raspberry worsted, and there was a plume of white feathers. Gloves were chamois with gauntlet cuffs. Waistbelts (poyas) were of white linen (kholshchevyi) in the 1st or Leib Squadron, and dark-blue polished linen (krasheninnyi) in the 2nd or Staff (Shtabskii) Squadron (Illus. No. 1185). Weaponry and accouterments consisted of: saber, with steel or iron hilt and black scabbard with iron fittings, carried on a waistbelt (poyas) of black unfinished leather straps; pistols, with brass fittins, carried hanging from an iron hook on a deerskin bandolier (pantaler) or crossbelt (pogonnaya perevyaz'), whose buckle, prong, and end piece were of brass; cartridge pouch (lyadunka), of hussar pattern except for being a little smaller; iron lance (pika), with a red painted shaft. The saddle had a red cloth pillow and no holsters; the saddlecloth was of red cloth trimmed around the edges and diagonally across the corners with white tape; white cloth valise; all horse furniture straps black; iron buckles and rings (Illus. 1185) [81].

While wearing the exact same uniform as prescribed for private Leib-Cossacks, non-commissioned officers did not have the crossbelt, cartridge pouch, and lance, and instead of a single pistol had two placed in holsters as in the regular cavalry. In each of these holsters were six cartridge pockets. In dismounted order all that distinguished Leib-Cossack non-commissioned officers from privates was that the former had canes (Illus. 1186) [82].

Trumpeters had uniform clothing and weaponry exactly as for non-commissioned officers, but with the addition of crimson cloth swallows' nests and yellow worsted sewn-on stripes. Their trumpets were brass with cords and tassels of yellow and crimson worsted (Illus. 1186) [83].

The staff-trumpeter was distinguished from the preceding squadron trumpeters only in that he had a cane (Illus. 1186) [84].

Officers had half-caftans with silver buttonhole loops (petlitsy), of galloon with small tassels of twisted fringe (iz vitoi kaniteli). Sabertaches had silver tassels and cords. Sabers had the swordknots authorized for all cavalry officers. Belts for sabers were of red morocco leather (Illus. 1187). Two pistols were carried when mounted. Their saddlecloths were the same as for lower ranks but trimmed with silver galloon [85].

The Leib-Cossack uniform described here was for summer. During the rest of the year all the above-mentioned ranks wore, over the red half-caftans, very dark-blue (temno-sinii) cloth caftans (kaftany) reaching halfway down the calf and with a standing collar (Illus. 1188). For lower ranks these caftans had no trim of any kind, but for officers they had narrow silver galloon down the front opening and around the collar. Also, they had silver buttonhole loops on the chest, with small fringed tassels (Illus. 1188) [86]. For cold or inclement weather all ranks were authorized white cloth cloaks (plashchi) [87].

1798 July 10 – Noncombatant Leib-Cossack ranks, such as: medics (fel'dshera), gunstock maker (lozhennyi master), metalsmith (slesar'), farrier (konoval), blacksmith (kuznets), and provost (profos), as well as the quartermaster (kvartermistr), legal assisant (auditor), and doctor (lekar'), were prescribed all the same uniform clothing as these ranks had in regular cavalry regiments [88].

NOTES

(1) Chronicle of the Russian IMPERIAL Army, compiled by Prince Dolgorukov and issued by HIGHESTOrder, St. Petersburg, 1797, No. 1; HIGHEST confirmed table of uniforms, accouterments, and weaponry for the Life-Guards Preobrazhenskii, Semenovskii, and Izmailovskii Regiments, 10 July 1798; drawings located in HIS IMPERIAL MAJESTY's Own Library catalogued under Nos. 158 and 159, and statements by contemporaries.

(2) The tables mentioned in the preceding note, and actual halberds preserved in various arsenals.

(3) According to the tables mentioned above in Note 1, halberd shafts were to be the same color as flag poles, but the latter, as can be seen from drawings in HIS IMPERIAL MAJESTY's Own Library under No 158, were coffee-colored.

(4) The tables mentioned above in Note 1.

(5) The tables of 10 July 1798 mentioned above in Note 1, and the drawings of No 158.

(6) The tables mentioned above in Note 1, and a general note confirmed 17 February 1797 by HIGHEST Authority for the Commissariat regarding infantry uniforms.

(7) The tables mentioned above in Note 1 and statements by contemporaries.

(8) Chronicle of the Russian IMPERIAL Army, compiled by Prince Dolgorukov, Nos. 1, 3, and 5; tables and drawings under Nos 158 and 159, mentioned above in Note 1, and statements by contemporaries.

(9) The tables mentioned above in Note 1.

(10) A general note confirmed 17 February 1797 by HIGHEST Authority for the Commissariat regarding infantry uniforms, and statements by contemporaries.

(11) Short Historical Journal of the Life-Guards Semenovskii Regiment, compiled by the regiment in 1825.

(12) Chronicle of the Russian Army, compiled by Prince Dolgorukov, Nos. 2, 4 and 6.

(13) Ibid.

(14) Ibid., and statements by contemporaries.

(15) Chronicle of the Russian Army, compiled by Prince Dolgorukov, No. 5, and HIGHEST confirmed tables of uniforms, accouterments, and weaponry for the Life-Guards Preobrazhenskii, Semenovskii, and Izmailovskii Regiments, 10 July 1798.

(16) Chronicle of the Russian Army, compiled by Prince Dolgorukov, Nos. 1, 3, and 5, Complete Collection of Laws of the Russian Empire (Polnoe Sobranie Zakonov Rossiiskoi Imperii, hereafter PSZ), Vol. XXV, No 18,790, pg. 486; actual grenadier caps and officers' gorgets in HIS IMPERIAL MAJESTY's Own Arsenal, and statements by contemporaries.

(17) Chronicle of the Russian Army, compiled by Prince Dolgorukov, Nos. 1, 2, 3, 4, and 6, the tables cited above in Note 15, and statements by contemporaries.

(18) PSZ, Vol. XXV, No 19,075, pg. 755; Chronicle of the Russian Army, compiled by Prince Dolgorukov, Nos. 2, 4, and 6, and actual grenadier caps in HIS IMPERIAL MAJESTY's Own Arsenal.

(19) Chronicle of the Russian Army, compiled by Prince Dolgorukov, No. 2.

(20) PSZ, Vol. XLIV, Part II, section four, under information on uniforms, page 3, No 19,178, and statements by contemporaries.

(21) Drawings located in HIS IMPERIAL MAJESTY's Own Library catalogued under No. 177, sheets 1, 2, 3, 4, 5, and 6; table of uniforms of Russian forces, March 1800, compiled by Major General Prince Dolgorukov and located in the SOVEREIGN EMPEROR's Library, catalogued under No 327; actual uniform clothing preserved in the personal arsenals of HIS IMPERIAL MAJESTY THE SOVEREIGN EMPEROR and HIS IMPERIAL HIGHNESS GRAND DUKE MICHAEL PAVLOVICH , and statements by contemporaries.

(22) Ditto.

(23) Ditto.

(24) Ditto.

(25) Ditto.

(26) Actual uniform preserved in HIS IMPERIAL HIGHNESS GRAND DUKE MICHAEL PAVLOVICH 's Own Arsenal, and statements by contemporaries.

(27) Actual coat and hat preserved in the armory of the Life-Guards Preobrazhenskii Regiment, and statements by contemporaries.

(28) Actual drum preserved in the SOVEREIGN EMPEROR's Own Arsenal, and statements by contemporaries.

(29) Drawings located in HIS IMPERIAL MAJESTY's Own Library catalogued under Nos. 158 and 159; Chronicle of the Russian Army, compiled by Prince Dolgorukov, No. 225, and a HIGHEST Confirmed table of uniforms, accouterments, and weapons for the Jäger battalion, 10 July 1798.

(30) HIGHEST Confirmed tables of uniforms, accouterments, and weapons for the Life-Guards Garrison Battalion, 29 July 1799 and 10 July 1800; grenadier caps of this battalion, preserved in IMPERIAL MAJESTY's Own Arsenal, and statements by contemporaries.

(31) Ditto.

(32) Ditto.

(33) Drawings located in HIS IMPERIAL MAJESTY's Own Library, and statements by contemporaries.

(34) Ditto.

(35) Ditto.

(36) Ditto.

(37) Ditto.

(38) Actual supervests and parade horse harness preserved in the personal arsenals of HIS IMPERIAL MAJESTY THE SOVEREIGN EMPEROR and HIS IMPERIAL HIGHNESS GRAND DUKE MICHAEL PAVLOVICH .

(39) Drawings located in HIS IMPERIAL MAJESTY's Own Library under No. 159; actual armor, gauntlets, thigh pieces, and shishka helmet preserved in HIS IMPERIAL MAJESTY's Own Arsenal, in the Anichkov Palace, and statements by contemporaries.

(40) HIGHEST confirmed table of uniforms, accouterments, and weapons for the Cavalier Guards Corps, 6 April 1799; also a table of uniforms from March 1800 compiled by Major General Prince Dolgorukov and locacted in HIS IMPERIAL MAJESTY's Own Library under No 327.

(41) Ditto.

(42) Ditto.

(43) Chronicle of the Russian Army, compiled by Prince Dolgorukov, No. 160; drawings in HIS IMPERIAL MAJESTY's Own Library, as mentioned in the preceding three notes.

(44) HIGHEST Confirmed table of uniforms, accouterments, and weapons for the Cavalier Guards Corps, 6 August 1799; Chronicle of the Russian Army, compiled by Prince Dolgorukov, No. 160; by the same Prince Dolgorukov, table of uniforms, March 1800, located in HIS IMPERIAL MAJESTY's Own Library under No 327, and statements by contemporaries.

(45) The same sources as in the preceding note, and also an actual helmet preserved in HIS IMPERIAL MAJESTY's Own Arsenal, in the Anichkov Palace.

(46) The same sources as in Note 43, and also an actual undress coat preserved in HIS IMPERIAL HIGHNESS GRAND DUKE MICHAEL PAVLOVICH 's Own Arsenal.

(47) The same sources as in Note 43.

(48) Ditto.

(49) Ditto.

(50) The table cited in Note 43, and actual papers regarding the uniforms for the Cavalier Guards Corps, preserved in the Moscow Section of the Archive of the War Ministry's Inspection Department.

(51) The same sources as in Note 43.

(52) Table of uniforms, March 1800, cited above in Notes 40, 41, and 42.

(53) HIGHESTConfirmed table of uniforms, accouterments, and weapons for the Cavalier Guards Corps, 15

May 1800; actual items preserved in the personal arsenals of HIS IMPERIAL MAJESTY THE SOVEREIGN EMPEROR and HIS IMPERIAL HIGHNESS GRAND DUKE MICHAEL PAVLOVICH ; and statements by contemporaries.

(54) Ditto.

(55) Ditto.

(56) Ditto.

(57) Actual papers regarding the uniforms for the Cavalier Guards Corps in 1800, preserved in the Moscow Section of the Archive of the War Ministry's Inspection Department; an officer's uniform preserved in HIS IMPERIAL HIGHNESS GRAND DUKE MICHAEL PAVLOVICH 's Own Arsenal.

(58) The papers cited in the preceding note, and the table cited in Notes 53, 54, 55, and 56.

(59) The same papers and statements by contemporaries. In HIS IMPERIAL HIGHNESS GRAND DUKE MICHAEL PAVLOVICH 's Own Arsenal is an undress coat of the Life-Guards Horse Regiment from this time, of the same pattern as for the Cavalier Guards except with dark-blue lapels and cuffs instead of green, and gold buttons instead of silver.

(60) Drawings of guards coats in HIS IMPERIAL MAJESTY's Own Library catalogued under No 158, and a HIGHESTConfirmed table of uniforms, accouterments, and weapons for the Life-Guards Horse Regiment, 10 July 1798.

(61) Chronicle of the Russian Army, compiled by Prince Dolgorukov, No. 161, and statements by contemporaries.

(62) Chronicle of the Russian Army, compiled by Prince Dolgorukov, No. 161, and an actual officer's undress uniform preserved in HIS IMPERIAL HIGHNESS GRAND DUKE MICHAEL PAVLOVICH's Own Arsenal.

(63) Complete Collection of Laws of the Russian Empire (Polnoe Sobranie Zakonov Rossiiskoi Imperii, hereafter PSZ), Vol. XXIV, No 18,837, pg. 548, and statements by contemporaries.

(64) PSZ, Vol. XLIV, Part II, Sect. Four, under information on uniforms page 3, No. 19,178, and statements by contemporaries.

(65) HIGHESTConfirmed table of uniforms, accouterments, and weapons, 2 February 1800, and table of of uniforms, March 1800, compiled by Major General Prince Dolgorukov, in HIS IMPERIAL MAJESTY's Own Library catalogued under No 327.

(66) Statements by contemporaries and an actual undress coat preserved HIS IMPERIAL HIGHNESS GRAND DUKE MICHAEL PAVLOVICH's Own Arsenal.

(67) HIGHESTConfirmed table of uniforms, accouterments, and weapons for the Leib-Hussar-Cossack Regiment, 13 December 1796; drawings in HIS IMPERIAL MAJESTY's Own Library catalogued under Nos 158 and 159; actual Leib-Hussar uniform clothing preserved in HIS IMPERIAL HIGHNESS GRAND DUKE MICHAEL PAVLOVICH's Own Arsenal, , and statements by contemporaries.

(68) The table cited in the preceding note, and statements by contemporaries.

(69) Ditto.

(70) The drawings cited above in Note 67; barsyand sarsamypreserved in the personal arsenals of HIS IMPERIAL MAJESTY THE SOVEREIGN EMPEROR and HISIMPERIALHIGHNESSGRANDDUKEMICHAELPAVLOVICH; and statements by contemporaries.

(71) The table and drawings cited above in Note 67, and statements by contemporaries.

(72) The same tabel and statements.

(73) HIGHESTConfirmed table of uniforms, accouterments, and weapons for the Leib-Hussar Regiment, 10 July 1798.

(74) Ukase from the Government Military Collegium to the Commissariat Department, 13 October 1798.

(75) A similar ukase of 20 October 1798, and statements by contemporaries.

(76) Chronicle of the Russian Army, compiled by Prince Dolgorukov, No. 246, and statements by contemporaries.

(77) PSZ Vol. XXIV, No 18,837, pg. 548, and statements by contemporaries.

(78) PSZ, Vol. XLIV, Part II, Sect. Four, under information on uniforms page 3, No 19,178, and statements by contemporaries.

(79) Ukase from the Government Military Collegium to the Commissariat Department, 22 November 1799.

(80) A similar ukase of 11 June 1800.

(81) HIGHESTConfirmed table of uniforms, accouterments, and weapons for the Leib-Hussar-Cossack Regiment, 13 December 1796; drawings in HIS IMPERIAL MAJESTY's Own Library catalogued under Nos 158, 159, and 327; Chronicle of the Russian Army, compiled by Prince Dolgorukov, No 203, and statements by contemporaries.

(82) The table cited in the preceding note, and statements by contemporaries.

(83) Ditto.

(84) Ditto.

(85) The drawings cited in Note 81; Chronicle of the Russian Army, compiled by Prince Dolgorukov, No 213, and statements by contemporaries.

(86) The same sources as cited in Note 81.

(87) Ditto.

(88) HIGHEST Confirmed table of uniforms, accouterments, and weapons for the Leib-Cossack Regiment, 10 July 1798.

РИСУНКИ
Одежды и Вооруженія
РОССІЙСКИХЪ
ВОЙСКЪ.

PLATES LIST OF ILLUSTRATIONS

1119. Musketeers. Life-Guards Preobrazhenskii, Semenovskii, and Izmailovskii Regiments, 1796-1797.

1120. Musketeer Non-Commissioned Officer. Life-Guards Preobrazhenskii Regiment, 1796-1797.

1121. Musketeer Drummer. Life-Guards Izmailovskii Regiment, 1796-1797.

1122. Grenadiers. Life-Guards Preobrazhenskii, Semenovskii, and Izmailovskii Regiments, 1796-1797.

1123. Cap plate and band for Grenadier caps in the Life-Guards Preobrazhenskii, Semenovskii, and Izmailovskii Regiments, 1797-1798.

1124. Drummer and Fifer. Grenadier companies of the Life-Guards Izmailovskii and Semenovskii Regiments, 1796-97.

1125. Musician. Life-Guards Semenovskii Regiment, 1796-1797.

1126. Company-Grade Officers. Life-Guards Preobrazhenskii, Semenovskii, and Izmailovskii Regiments, 1796-1797.

1127. Musketeer. Life-Guards Izmailovskii Regiment, 1797.

1128. Non-Commissioned Officers. Life-Guards Preobrazhenskii and Semenovskii Regiments, 1797.

1129. Company-Grade Officers. Life-Guards Preobrazhenskii and Izmailovskii Regiments, 1797-1799.

1130. Cap plate for Grenadier caps in the Life-Guards Preobrazhenskii, Semenovskii, and Izmailovskii Regiments, 1798-1799, and medallion (medalion) for officers' gorgets of the same regiments, 1798-1801.

1131. Cap plate and band for Grenadier caps in the Life-Guards Preobrazhenskii, Semenovskii, and Izmailovskii Regiments, 1799-1801.

1132. Grenadier. Life-Guards Preobrazhenskii Regiment, 1800-1801.

1133. Guards Grenadier Caps, 1800. aa. Preobrazhenskii Regiment, bb. Semenovskii Regiment, cc. Izmailovskii Regiment.

1134. Field-Grade Officers of the Life-Guards Izmailovskii and Semenovskii Regiments, 1800-1801, and of the Preobrazhenskii Regiment, 1800.

1135. Officers' coat embroidery in Life-Guards regiments; a. Preobrazhenskii, 1800; b. Semenovskii, 1800 and 1801; c. Izmailovskii, 1800 and 1801; d. Preobrazhenskii, 1800 and 1801.

1136. Company Grade Officers. Life-Guards Preobrazhenskii Regiment, 1800-1801.

1137. Fifers. Leib-Battalion of the Life-Guards Preobrazhenskii Regiment, 1800-1801.

1138. Turkish drum, 1800-1801.

1139. Non-Commissioned Officer and Private. Life-Guards Jäger Battalion, 1796-1801.

1140. Staff-Waldhornist and Waldhornist. Life-Guards Jäger Battalion, 1796-1801.

1141. Company-Grade Officer. Life-Guards Jäger Battalion, 1796-1801.

1142. Grenadier and Company-Grade Officer. Life-Guards Garrison Battalion, 1799-1801.

1143. Private. Cavalier Guards Squadrons, 1797.

1144. Non-Commissioned Officer. Cavalier Guards Squadrons, 1797.

1145. Trumpeter. Cavalier Guards Squadrons, 1797.

1146. Officer. Cavalier Guards Squadrons, 1797.

1147. Officer. Cavalier Guards Squadrons, 1797.

1148. Cavalier-Guards Supervest, 1797.

1149. Parts of the horse harness for Cavalier-Guards officers, 1797, 1799, and 1801.

1150. Cavalier-Guards Cuirasses, 1797, 1800, and 1801.

1151-1152. Cavalier-Guards Shishki Helmets, 1797.

1153. Private. Cavalier Guards Corps, 1799-1800. (In everyday uniform.)

1154. Trumpeter and NCO Cavalier Guards Corps, 1799. (In everyday uniform.)

1155. Officers. Cavalier Guards Corps, 1799. (In everyday uniform.)

1156. NCO Officer. Cavalier Guards Corps, 1799. (In parade uniform.)

1157-1158. Cavalier-Guards Helmets (Kaski), 1799.

1159. Private, Non-Commissioned Officer, and Trumpeter. Cavalier Guards Corps, 1799-1800. (In undress coat (vitse-mundir).)

1160. Officer. Cavalier Guards Corps, 1799. (In undress coat (vitse-mundir).)

1161. Cavalier-Guards Supervest, 1800.

1162. Officer. Cavalier Guards Corps, 1800. (In undress coat.)

1163. Private. Cavalier Guards Regiment, 1800-1801.

1164. Non-Commissioned Officer and Trumpeter. Cavalier Guards Regiment, 1800-1801. (In everyday uniform.)

1165. Officer. Cavalier Guards Regiment, 1800-1801.

1166. Officer. Cavalier Guards Regiment, 1800-1801. (In undress coat.)

1167. Private. Life-Guards Horse Regiment, 1796-1801. (1st Squadron.)

1168. NCO Life-Guards Horse Regiment, 1796-1801. (2nd, 3rd, and 4th Squadrons.)

1169. Trumpeter. Life-Guards Horse Regiment, 1796-1801. (5th Squadron.)

1170. Officers. Life-Guards Horse Regiment, 1796-1801. (1st, 2nd and 3rd Squadrons.)

1171. Officers. Life-Guards Horse Regiment, 1796-1801. (4th and 5th Squadrons.)

1172. Officer. Life-Guards Horse Regiment, 1796-1798. (In undress coat.)

1173. Officer. Life-Guards Horse Regiment, 1799. (In undress coat.)

1174. Officers' embroidery on undress coat, Life-Guards Horse Regiment, 1799.

Musketeers. Life-Guards Preobrazhenskii, Semenovskii, and Izmailovskii Reg. 1796-1797.

1120.

Составил Землянченко и Захаровъ.   Рис. на кам. Бѣлоусовъ.

Musketeer Non-Commissioned Officer. Life-Guards Preobrazhenskii Regiment, 1796-1797.

Musketeer Drummer. Life-Guards Izmailovskii Regiment, 1796-1797.

1122.

Grenadiers. Life-Guards Preobrazhenskii, Semenovskii, and Izmailovskii Reg. 1796-1797.

Cap plate and band for Grenadier caps in the Life-Guards Preobrazhenskii, Semenovskii, and
Izmailovskii Regiments, 1797-1798.

Drummer and Fifer. of the Life-Guards Izmailovskii and Semenovskii Regiments, 1796-97.

Musician. Life-Guards Semenovskii Regiment, 1796-1797.

Officers. Life-Guards Preobrazhenskii, Semenovskii, and Izmailovskii Regiments, 1796-1797.

Musketeer. Life-Guards Izmailovskii Regiment, 1797.

Non-Commissioned Officers. Life-Guards Preobrazhenskii and Semenovskii Regiments, 1797.

Officers. Life-Guards Preobrazhenskii and Izmailovskii Regiments, 1797-1799.

Cap plate for Grenadier caps in the Life-Guards Preobrazhenskii, Semenovskii, and Izmailovskii Regiments, 1798-1799, and medallion for officers' gorgets of the same regiments, 1798-1801.

1131.

Cap plate and band for Grenadier caps in the Life-Guards Preobrazhenskii, Semenovskii, and Izmailovskii Regiments, 1799-1801.

1132.

Составл. Пиратскій.   Рис на кам. Бѣлоусовъ и Байеръ.

Grenadier. Life-Guards Preobrazhenskii Regiment, 1800-1801.

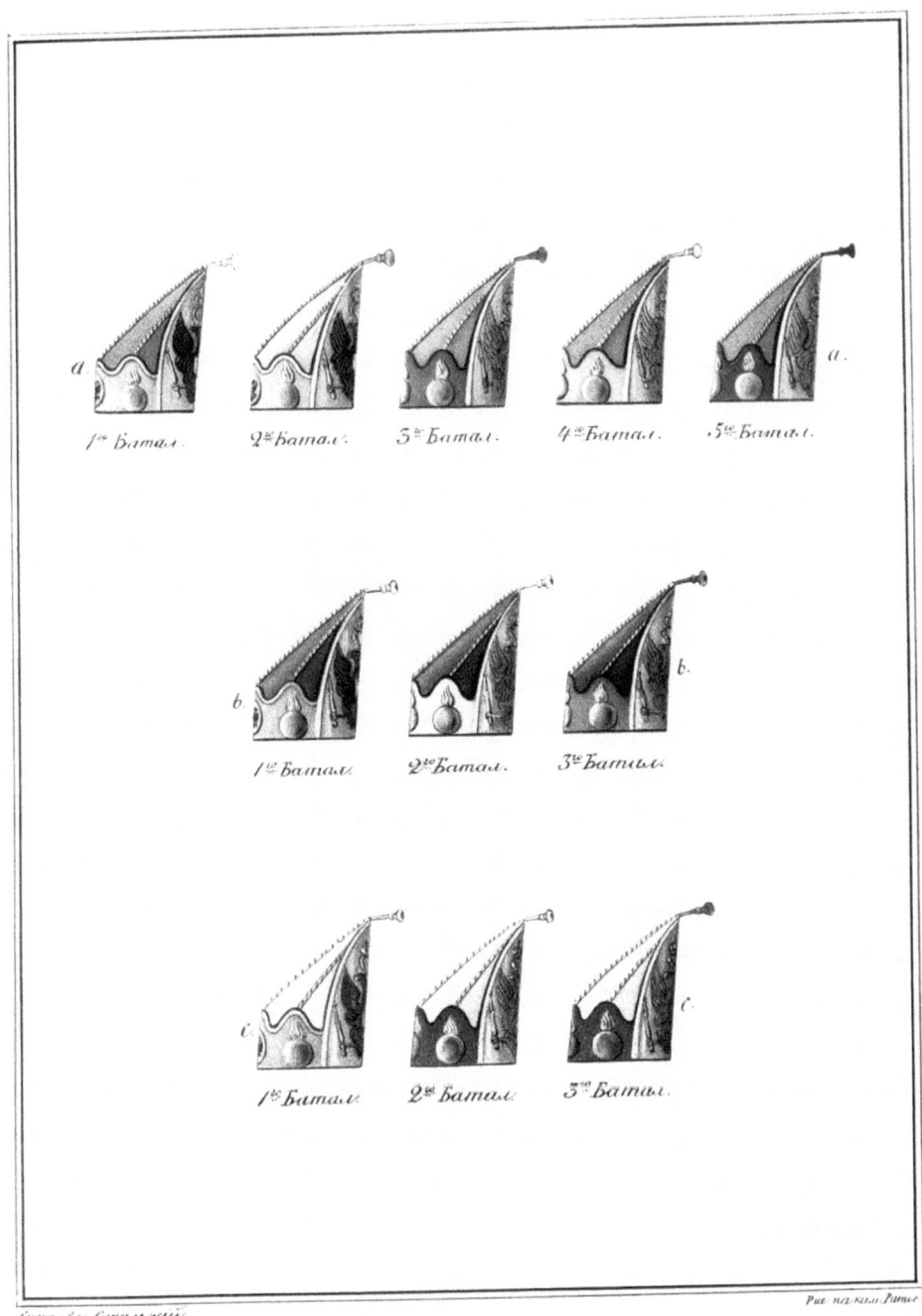

Guards Grenadier Caps, 1800. aa. Preobrazhenskii Regiment, bb. Semenovskii Regiment, cc.
Izmailovskii Regiment.

Field-Grade Officers of the Life-Guards Izmailovskii and Semenovskii Regiments, 1800-1801, and of the Preobrazhenskii Regiment, 1800.

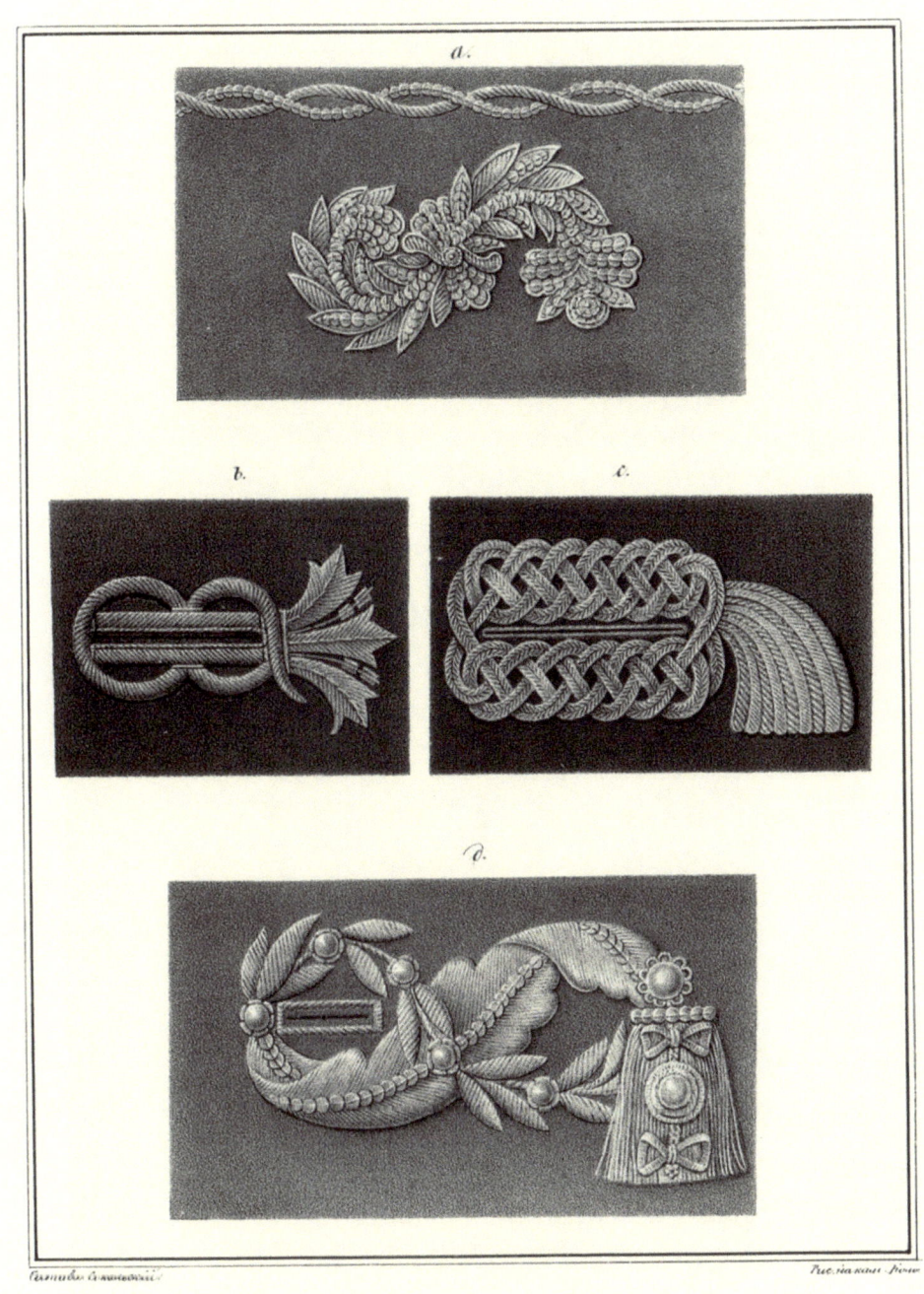

a.

b. *c.*

д.

Officers' coat embroidery in Life-Guards regiments; a. Preobrazhenskii, 1800; b. Semenovskii, 1800 and 1801; c. Izmailovskii, 1800 and 1801; d. Preobrazhenskii, 1800 and 1801.

Company-Grade Officers. Life-Guards Preobrazhenskii Regiment, 1800-1801.

Fifers. Leib-Battalion of the Life-Guards Preobrazhenskii Regiment, 1800-1801.

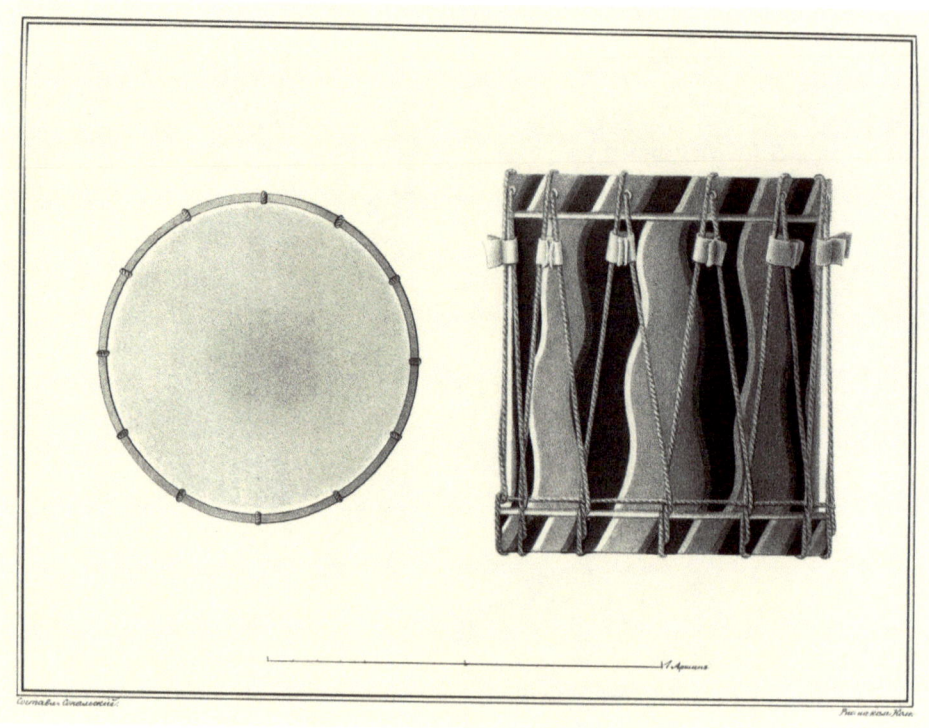

Turkish drum, 1800-1801.

Non-Commissioned Officer and Private. Life-Guards Jäger Battalion, 1796-1801.

Staff-Waldhornist and Waldhornist. Life-Guards Jäger Battalion, 1796-1801.

1741.

Company-Grade Officer. Life-Guards Jäger Battalion, 1796-1801.

1142.

Grenadier and Company-Grade Officer. Life-Guards Garrison Battalion, 1799-1801.

Private. Cavalier Guards Squadrons, 1797.

Non-Commissioned Officer. Cavalier Guards Squadrons, 1797.

Trumpeter. Cavalier Guards Squadrons, 1797.

Officer. Cavalier Guards Squadrons, 1797.

Officer. Cavalier Guards Squadrons, 1797.

1148.

1150.

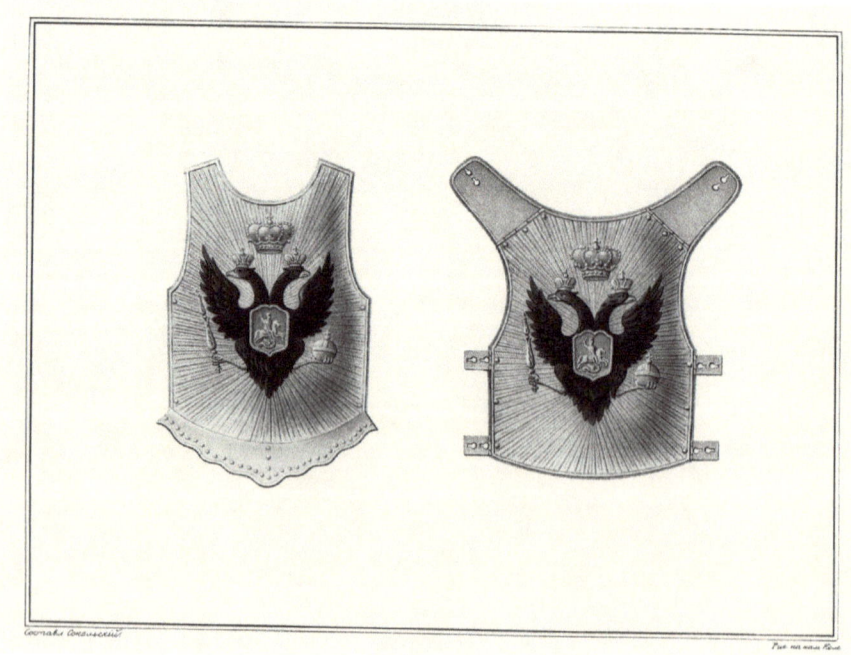

Cavalier-Guards Supervest, 1797.   Cavalier-Guards Cuirasses, 1797, 1800, and 1801.

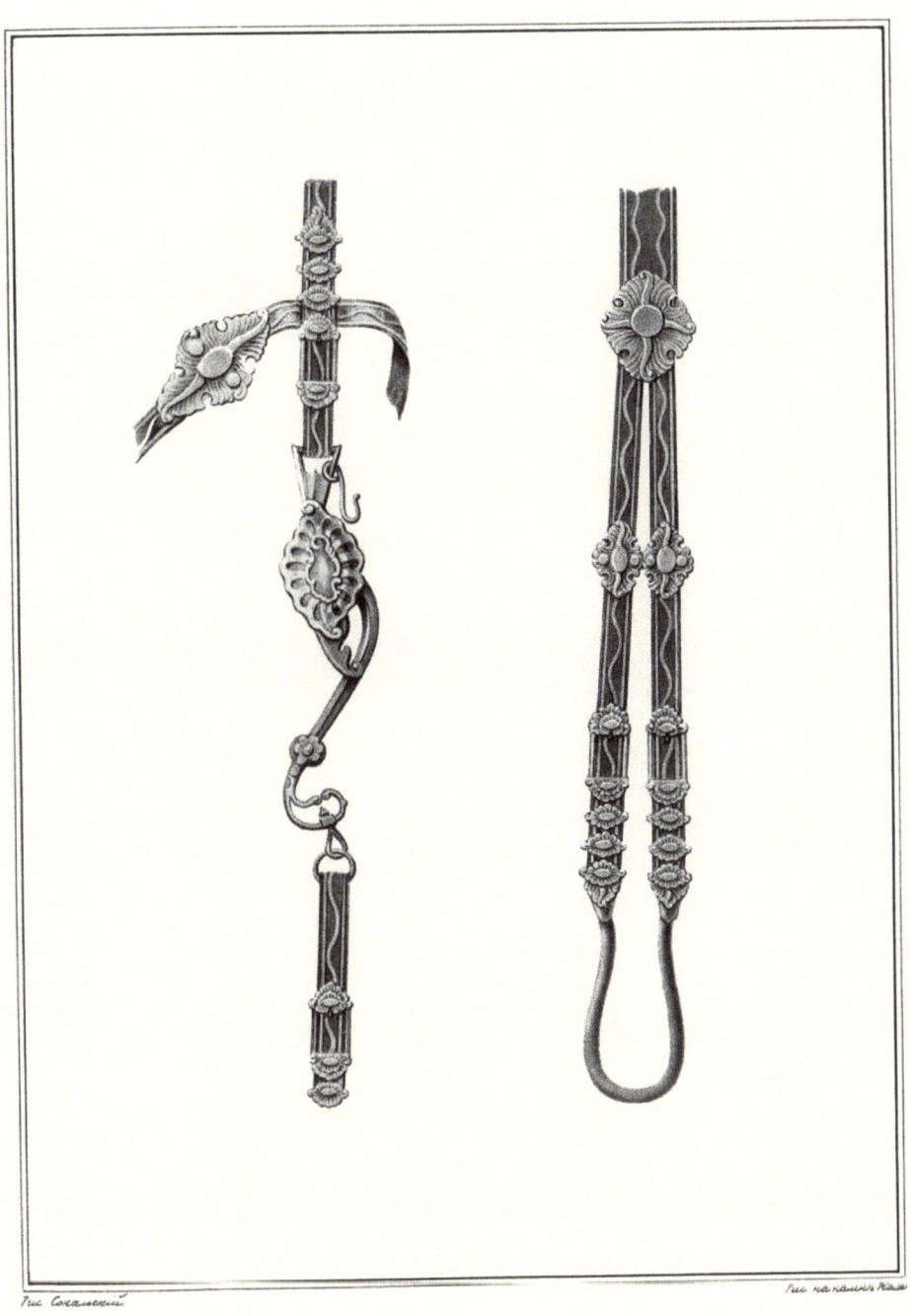

Parts of the horse harness for Cavalier-Guards officers, 1797, 1799, and 1801.

Cavalier-Guards Shishki Helmets, 1797.

Cavalier-Guards Shishki Helmets, 1797.

Private. Cavalier Guards Corps, 1799-1800. (In everyday uniform.)

Trumpeter and NCO. Cavalier Guards Corps, 1799. (In everyday uniform.)

Officers. Cavalier Guards Corps, 1799. (In everyday uniform.)

Officer and Non-Commissioned Officer. Cavalier Guards Corps, 1799. (In parade uniform.)

Cavalier-Guards Helmets (Kaski), 1799.

Cavalier-Guards Helmets (Kaski), 1799.

Private, NCO, and Trumpeter. Cavalier Guards Corps, 1799-1800. (In undress coat)

Officer. Cavalier Guards Corps, 1799. (In undress coat (vitse-mundir).)

Cavalier-Guards Supervest, 1800.

Officer. Cavalier Guards Corps, 1800. (In undress coat.)

Private. Cavalier Guards Regiment, 1800-1801.

NCO and Trumpeter. Cavalier Guards Regiment, 1800-1801. (In everyday uniform.)

Officer. Cavalier Guards Regiment, 1800-1801.

Officer. Cavalier Guards Regiment, 1800-1801. (In undress coat.)

Private. Life-Guards Horse Regiment, 1796-1801. (1st Squadron.)

NCO. Life-Guards Horse Regiment, 1796-1801. (2nd, 3rd, and 4th Squadrons.)

1169.

Trumpeter. Life-Guards Horse Regiment, 1796-1801. (5th Squadron.)

Officers. Life-Guards Horse Regiment, 1796-1801. (1st, 2nd and 3rd Squadrons.)

Officers. Life-Guards Horse Regiment, 1796-1801. (4th and 5th Squadrons.)

Officer. Life-Guards Horse Regiment, 1796-1798. (In undress coat.)

Officer. Life-Guards Horse Regiment, 1799. (In undress coat.)

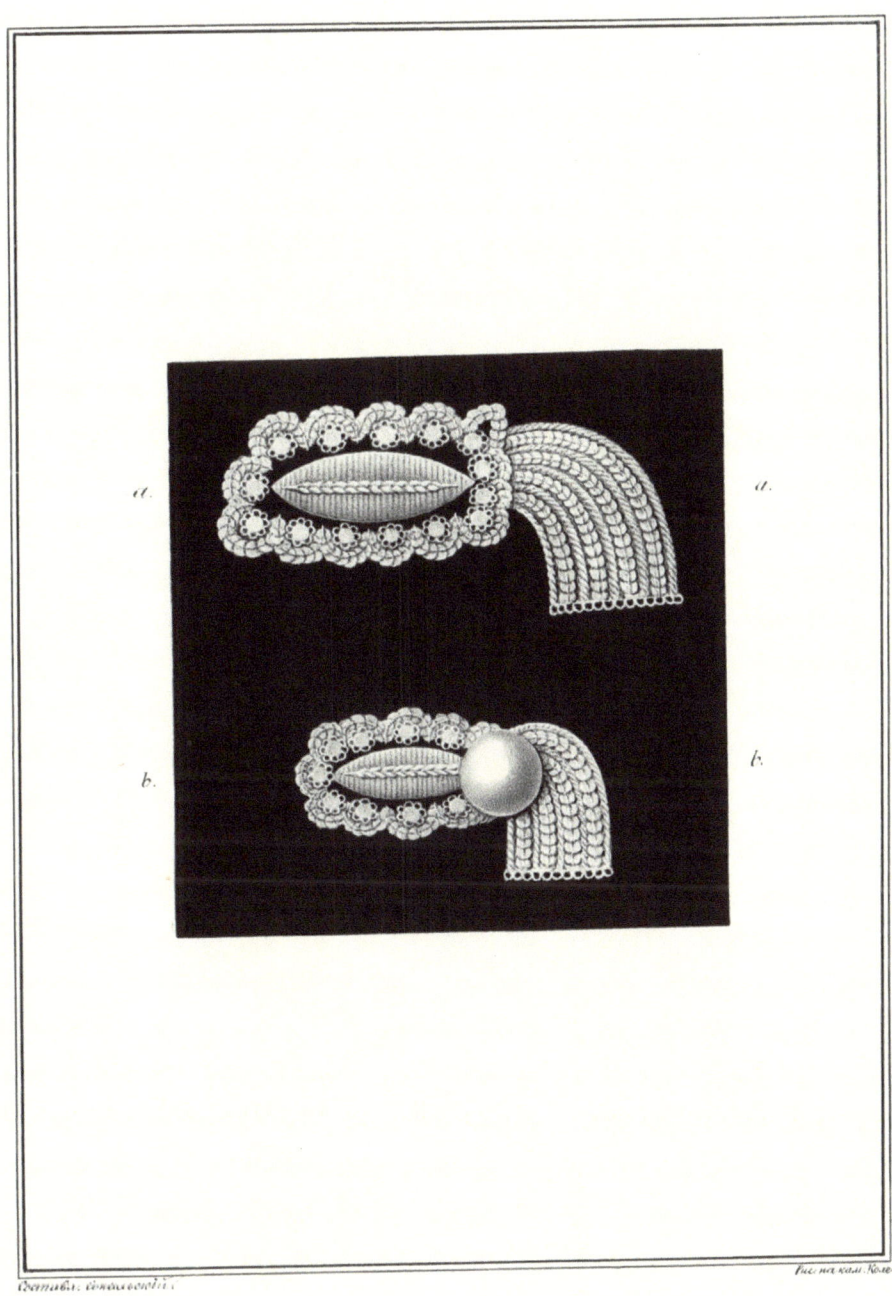

Officers' embroidery on undress coat, Life-Guards Horse Reg., 1799. (a. on collar, b. on cuffs.)

WORK PLAN

Our reprint in based on the original 19th century volumes, to be precise the volumes from 7 to 9 are dedicated to the reign of Paul I; this first part is distributed on 7 volumes, having a numbering from 1 to 7. From number 10 to 18 of the original volumes, the second part is dedicated to the Russian troops under Alexander I. These still being worked on and they will be soon ready, distributed on twenty volumes approximately. Our new edition, the first ever published in English, both on paper and digital format, boasts a large number of color plates, many of them unpublished and coloured by our team of expert artists and scholars of uniformology. Each volume is based on 50/70 plates, always accompanied by the original translated text which describes the uniforms, the organization and the armament of the Russian army of the period.

 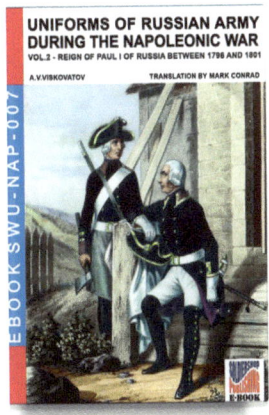 

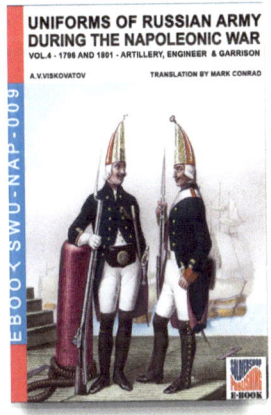 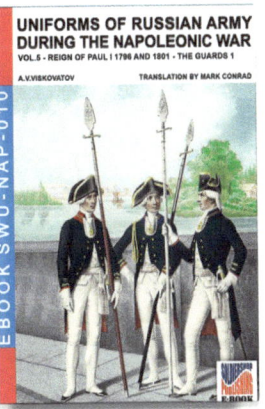  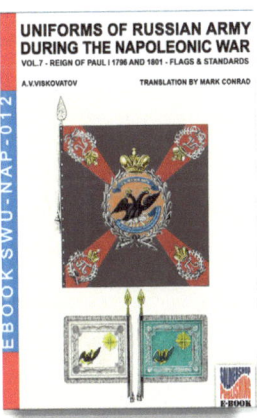

www.ingramcontent.com/pod-product-compliance
Lightning Source LLC
Chambersburg PA
CBHW041457120626
46547CB00003B/459